# THE MONKEYS'

# ABC

# WORD BOOK

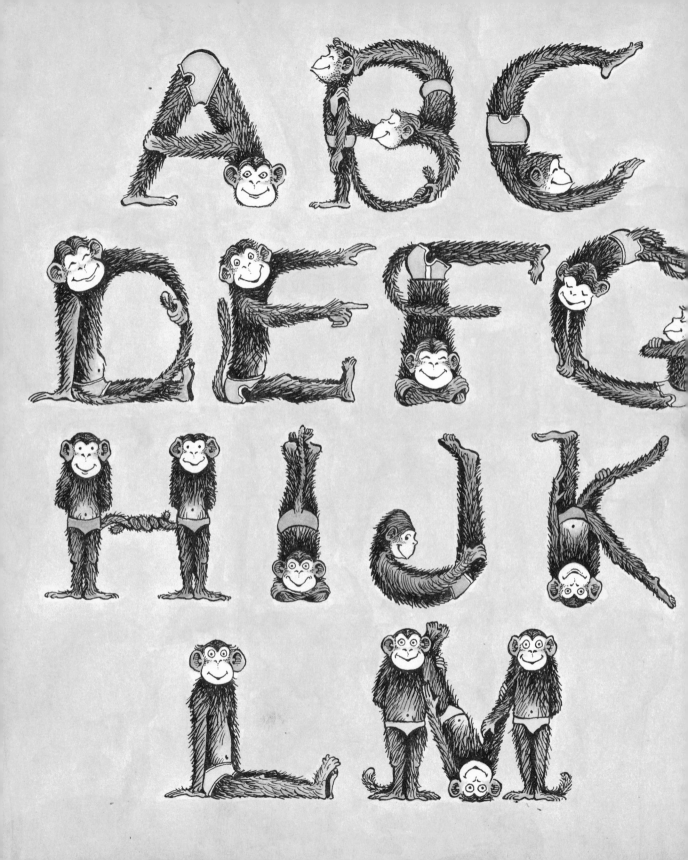

# THE MONKEYS'

# ABC

# WORD BOOK

## BY KELLY OECHSLI

GOLDEN PRESS • NEW YORK
Western Publishing Company, Inc., Racine, Wisconsin

aviator

apple

arrow

airplane

crocodile

coat

beetle

A B C

billboard

cap

bananas

A is for airplane.

B is for boat.

C for the crocodile, castle, and coat.

ants

cap

butterfly

belt

cat

birdcage

# DE

D is for dragon, dentist, and drill.
E for the elephant up on the hill.

DINER

door

drinking

doll

desk

doughnuts

eating

egg

dandelions

dog

eagle

ear

elephant

dragon

dentist

emu

donkey

daisies

elf

dancer

drum

elbow

hawk

FGH

horse

ghost

hog

hoe

fox

fruit

hen

frog

feather

goose

helicopter

helmet

football

flag

gate

house

farmer

hay

horn

goat

garden

hive

flowers

galoshes

grapes

HONEY

hornet

F is for farmer, fox, and frog.

G is for ghost.

H is for hog.

grasshopper

I is for ice skaters
playing ice hockey.

inchworm

igloo

injury

ICE CREAM

ICE CREAM
CONES · CUPS · STICKS

ice skaters

ice cream

jackdaw

**J** is for jaguar, juggler, and jockey.

Jill

jack-in-the-box

jellybeans

Jack

joker

jockey

jaguar

juggler

jar

jug

moon

mask

lamp

keys

K is for kettledrum, king, and kittens.

L is for lion.

M is for mittens.

mug

MONKEYS
MAGAZINE

marbles

kittens

mittens

lizard

# N

nest

nut

nightingale

newspaper

needles

noodles

napkins

nails

nine

net

newt

nozzle

oriole

owl

oboe

organ

oar

octopus

ocean

ostrich

orchestra

oysters

officer

BALTIMORE
ORIOLE

N is for newspaper, nails, and nine.

O for the ostrich with feathers so fine.

pennant

RIDES

PANTHER

pony

panther

pelican

PUBLIC PARK

P Q R

roses

rope

P is for pelican.

Q is for quail.

R for the raft going out for a sail.

rake

rat

rabbit

roller coaster

rain

PLAYLAND

peacock

robin

parrot

quail

rooster

uin

quetzal

pole

pond

raft

quilt

quart

pie

pear

picnic table

peas

pot

pan

pen

pencil

PICKLES

MILK

PRETZELS

pineapple

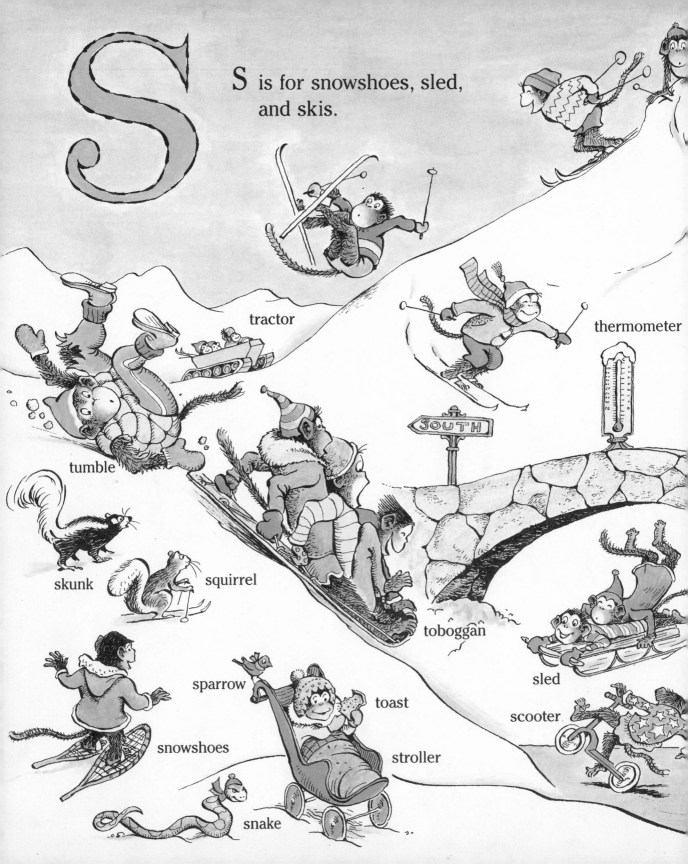

# S

S is for snowshoes, sled, and skis.

tractor

thermometer

tumble

SOUTH

skunk    squirrel

toboggan

sled

sparrow

toast

scooter

snowshoes

stroller

snake

sun

T for toboggan, tractor, and trees.

skis

tail

towline

trees

sleigh

SPORTS SHED & SHOP

snowman

skater

shovel

TENT SALE

stove

steps

# U
# V
# W

U is for uniform.
V is for vine.
W for the witch
with the valentine.

valen...

witch

vocalist

vase

ventriloquist

vine

wheelbarrow

ukelele

whistle

wrench

watch

waves

weather vane

umbrella

wren

violins

windmill

wall

wash

whale

WEST

uniform

vacuum cleaner

# X Y Z

X is for xylophone–it's fun to play.

Y for the yoke that the yaks wear all day.

Z is for zebra who lives in the zoo.

We know our alphabet; now, so do you!

xylophone

yoke

yaks

DO NOT FEED THE MONKEYS

zoo

zebra